P9-DHC-458

CHILDREN'S ROOM

AUG 1 1 1992

DATE DUE

SEP 2 2 1992	MAR 26 2002	
OCT 1 3 1992		
OCT 1 3 1992		
FEB 1 6 1993		
APR 1 7 1997		
AUG 1 4 1997		
JAN 1 3 1998		
FEB 1 1 1998		
DEC 0 5 2000		
FEB 0 8 2001		
DEC 1 1 2001		
NOV 1 8 2008		
FEB 0 5 2011		

Sand Dunes

Sand Dunes

A Carolrhoda Earth Watch Book

by Jan Gumprecht Bannan

Carolrhoda Books, Inc./Minneapolis

Photo on page 2: Winter's scouring winds sculpt patterns on these dunes in the Oregon Dunes National Recreation Area.

Thanks to Professor Robert E. Frenkel, Department of Geography, Oregon State University, and Professor Thomas A. Terich, Department of Geography and Regional Planning, Western Washington University, for their assistance with this book.

This edition of this book is available in two bindings:
Library binding by Carolrhoda Books, Inc.
Soft cover by First Avenue Editions
241 First Avenue North
Minneapolis, Minnesota 55401

LIBRARY OF CONGRESS CATALOGING-IN-PUBLICATION DATA

Bannan, Jan Gumprecht.
    Sand dunes: text and photographs / by Jan Gumprecht Bannan.
      p.   cm.
    "A Carolrhoda earth watch book."
    Summary: Discusses dune areas in Oregon and elsewhere in the western hemisphere, explaining the formation of sand and the forces which shape it into dunes.
    ISBN 0-87614-321-4 (lib. bdg.)
    ISBN 0-87614-513-6 (pbk.)
    1. Sand dunes—Juvenile literature. [1. Sand dunes.] I. Title.
GB632.B36 1989   87-27978
551.3'75—dc19   CIP
                          AC
Manufactured in the United States of America
2 3 4 5 6 7 8 9 10 99 98 97 96 95 94 93 92 91 90

Seasonal winds form curves in an oblique dune.

Throughout the world, there are places where the wind piles sand into strange and wonderful hills and ridges called dunes.

In many ways, all sand dunes are alike. They all need sand, wind, and space to form, and they all are constantly changing. However, each sand dune is also different from every other in some way. Its shape is determined by how much and what kind of sand is available to be blown into dunes, the direction and strength of the wind, how much plant growth is on or near the dune area, and how much water the dune area gets.

5

These California dune
formations are part of a
seemingly endless expanse
of sand.

Sand dunes can be found in coastal and inland deserts where large deposits of sand accumulate in dry, windy weather. Dunes can also form in nondesert conditions along the sandy shores of oceans, rivers, and lakes. However, not every one of these areas has the right combination of sand, wind, and space to form dunes.

Deserts are found on every continent. Deserts may be hot or cold, but they are always dry, because they receive little rain. With so little moisture, vegetation is scarce, and there is nothing to hold sand in place. In some areas, the sand is blown into tall, stark dunes that are part of a seemingly endless expanse of sand. They are an awe-inspiring sight to the few explorers who see them.

The largest desert area in the world, the Sahara Desert in northern Africa, covers 3½ million square miles (9 million sq km). Only part of this huge area contains sand dunes. In fact, dunes cover just 10 percent of the Sahara Desert.

The largest sea of sand in North America is the Gran Desierto of Sonora, Mexico, where windswept desert dunes vary from a few feet high to hundreds of feet high. In the United States, many dune systems are found in the inland desert country of the West. The highest dunes, almost 800 feet (244 m) tall, are in Great Sand Dunes National Monument in Colorado. Other desert dunes are in California's Death Valley and New Mexico's White Sands National Monument.

Where can you find dunes that are not in deserts? Look for them along coastlines where cliffs do not block their formation. In the United States, nondesert dunes exist on the shores of Lake Michigan and Lake Superior, and they also dot the east and west coasts of the country. On the Atlantic coast, Cape Cod, Massachusetts, and North Carolina have interesting sand dunes. Along the Pacific, several areas, including those on the Oregon coast, have beautiful dune formations.

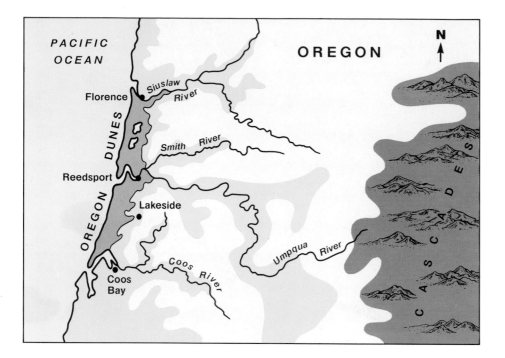

Sunset in the Oregon Dunes National Recreation Area brushes the sand with tints of orange and gold.

This book will focus on a dune area on the coast of Oregon. A close look at the geology, the weather, the sand supply, and the plant growth in this area will reveal many things about a coastal dune system.

Sand dunes cover 140 miles (225 km) of the Oregon shoreline. These golden hills rise up to 500 feet (152 m) above sea level, and they stretch as far as 2½ miles (4 km) inland.

The Cascade Mountain range provides pieces of rock that eventually find their way to the Oregon dunes in the form of sand.

Where does all this sand come from? Some of the sand that forms the Oregon dunes comes from Oregon's coastal cliffs. Other sand grains forming the Oregon dunes are tiny pieces of the different rocks that make up the Cascade Mountain range that stretches from northern California through Oregon and Washington and into southern British Columbia.

Wind, ice, and rain **weather** the rock, or break it down into smaller particles. These particles, called **sediments**, are carried to sea over waterfalls and down flowing streams and rivers. Some of these sediments are already sand and some will become sand as the water breaks the sediment into grains. Sand is defined by its size. Any **mineral** grains larger than dust but smaller than gravel are called sand. It may take thousands of years for sand to move 100 miles (160 km) down a river.

The Umpqua River in Oregon deposits sediments in the Pacific Ocean.

Oceans are great storehouses of sand. The Umpqua River is a major contributor of those sediments that are eventually tossed ashore by the waves of the Pacific Ocean and blown into the Oregon dunes. The Umpqua's source is Diamond Lake, high in the Cascade Mountains of Oregon. Many other rivers in the area—the Coquille, the Rogue, the Coos, the Siuslaw, and the Columbia—also add to the Pacific Ocean's supply of sand off the Oregon coast. In a process called **erosion**, winter rains and melting snow wash sediments down hills and mountainsides to rain-swollen rivers that, in turn, carry away even more sediments from their banks.

Once the sediments reach the Pacific Ocean, they are moved along the coast by the **current**, or the movement of water in a certain direction, and by winter storms. Seashells that waves have tumbled and broken into sand-sized grains are added to the sediments that have reached the ocean from the rivers.

Huge waves that sweep onto shore after a storm stir up sand from the bottom of the sea. These violent waves gradually erode the cliffs, particularly the softer ones, that edge areas of the Oregon coast. The cliff fragments add to the sediments in the ocean.

The surf gradually adds sediments to the ocean from cliffs along the coast.

A close look at beach sand reveals that each grain is a particle of a single mineral, which can be identified by its color.

Some sand from the ocean is tossed ashore by waves, forming beaches. This beach sand bears little resemblance to the rocks and shells it came from. Rivers and the ocean have broken the sediments into tiny grains. Each of these grains is a particle of a single mineral.

At the beach, a close look at a handful of sand reveals the various colors of the different minerals. The beach sand of the Oregon dunes area contains quite a lot of a milky white mineral called feldspar and colorless grains of a mineral called quartz. Iron minerals add contrasting colors of yellow, red, and brown. Garnet grains are a dark red color that is easy to spot, and grains of zircon that range from brown to almost no color glitter in the sunlight. The darker minerals are usually heavier than feldspar and quartz and are only occasionally blown into the dunes. The Oregon dunes are mostly made of quartz—the kind of sand familiar to anyone who has ever played in a sandbox. In the sunlight, the Oregon dunes look golden.

Gypsum sand forms the white dunes of White Sands National Monument, in New Mexico.

Not all dunes look like the Oregon dunes, however. Sand that is light enough to be blown into dunes can come from many different sources. In Hawaii, Bermuda, and Baja California, white calcite sand is made up of smooth grains of the shells of marine animals washed ashore from the ocean. White Sands National Monument, in New Mexico, has stunning white dunes of gypsum sand. This sand came from a dried-up lake bed, where huge quantities of the white mineral gypsum had been deposited.

Sand dunes do not form along this area of the coast where the inland movement of sand is blocked by cliffs.

High tides push sand far up on the shore. When the sand dries out, the wind can easily move it. Though travel through water has begun polishing the sand grains, they are shaped by the force of the wind. The wind blows the sand grains into obstacles and into each other, until they are tiny balls. They may stay that shape for millions of years. Sand grains between 0.1 mm and 1 mm in diameter (less than $\frac{1}{25}$ of an inch) seem to be the right weight for being blown into formations by the wind.

Enormous amounts of sand are needed to form tall sand dunes. At the Oregon coast where dunes are formed, sand is constantly washed ashore from the ocean, and the wind seldom stops picking up some of the sand and blowing it inland. In areas along the coast where there are high cliffs instead of low coastal plains, the movement of the sand inland is blocked by the cliffs, and no dunes will form.

Why doesn't the sand just spread out in a big sheet, like dust would? Particles of sand are larger and therefore heavier than dust particles. Winds of at least 10 miles per hour (16 km per hour) are needed to move sand grains, which are rarely lifted more than a foot or so off the ground. Even a fairly strong wind can keep sand grains in the air for only a few minutes, so sand does not float and scatter in all directions. If the sand lands on a hard surface, it bounces farther than if it lands on a soft surface, so sand tends to accumulate on soft surfaces. Dry sand dunes are soft, as anyone who has climbed one knows, so sand will pile up to form hills or ridges where there is already sand. Once a dune is formed, it does not stay put. Dunes are constantly moving and changing.

Late summer winds begin to rearrange transverse dune formations.

Wild winter storms can threaten the foredune.

Open expanses of sand undergo changes in appearance during the seasons of the year. The weather is mild year-round on the Oregon coast, but the seasons do change. Winter storms are wild. The blowing sand blasts everything from trees to dune formations. Sand avalanches pour down steep dunes, and lots of rain falls. However, some days in January are windless and sunny. On these days, the sand captures some of the sun's energy and reflects the rest, and the dunes become a warm, special landscape. Very little rain falls in the summer, but fog provides moisture to the sand.

Approaching the Oregon dunes from the west, the ocean side, the first dune formations one sees are the **foredunes**. These ridges developed after European beach grass was planted on the Oregon coast in the 1930s. Parallel to the beach and next to the winter highwater mark, the grasses trap blowing sand, and dunes build to heights of 25 to 35 feet (7-10 m).

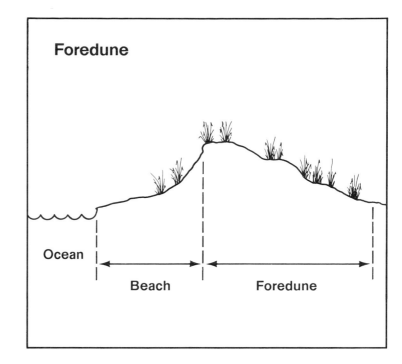

European beach grass causes a foredune to be formed at the beach line.

Deflation plains are found in low areas where the sand has been blown away and the water table has been exposed.

In many low places, shallow ponds of water appear where the sand has been blown away, exposing the **water table** beneath. These are called **deflation plains**. Deflation plains are found on the side of the foredunes that is farthest from the ocean and on the near ocean side of large moving dunes. During rainy winters, these wet areas get even wetter. Quicksand is sometimes found here, but it is not particularly hazardous.

Heading farther inland, one finds **transverse dunes**. In summer, the moderate northwest winds push the sand into small ridges about 6 feet (1.8 m) high. These transverse ridges form at right angles to the wind. The slope facing the wind rises gradually, and the side protected from the wind, called the **slip face**, drops off abruptly. Sand can be seen blowing along the top of the ridge, and some sand drops over the top of the ridge and falls down the steep slip face. Where there is enough open space, these ridges will be very long. If the wind isn't blocked by another dune, it may then scoop this sand up and form another transverse ridge, until several line up behind each other at distances of about 75 to 150 feet (23-46 m) apart. Transverse ridges are partly destroyed during winter by the southwest winds, but new ones form when the summer winds return.

The slip face is the steep side of a transverse ridge that is protected from the wind.

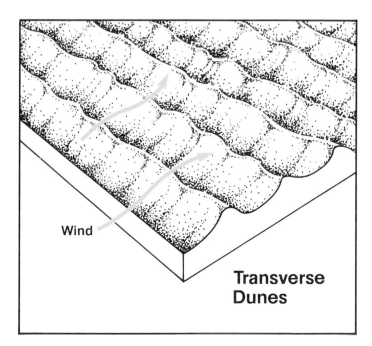

Wind

Transverse Dunes

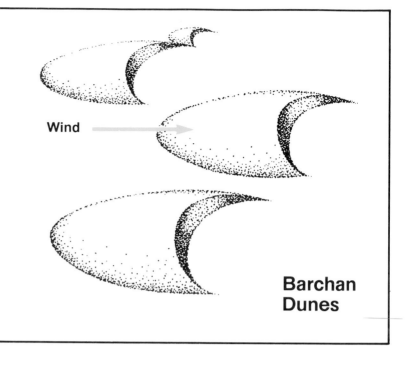

Wind

Barchan Dunes

Transverse ridges are found in many dune areas. Abundant sand and no plant growth to act as a barrier are necessary to their formation. In dune areas where there is less sand, obstructions such as vegetation and rocks are not buried. Sand that starts piling up on the obstructions builds into a dune formation called a **barchan dune**, which is shaped like a crescent moon. As the dune grows around the obstruction, sand grains are blown around the edges, producing "horns" that point away from the wind and give this formation its crescent shape. These dunes are sometimes huge.

The special summer and winter winds form oblique dunes, which are unique to Oregon.

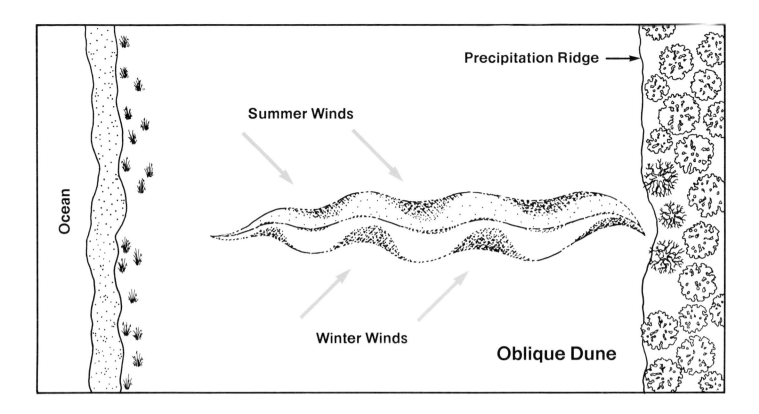

Winter storm winds in Oregon blow from the southwest, and they are stronger than the summer winds. Like giant hands, they reshape existing dunes and pile up sand around vegetation. Over a period of changing seasons, long **oblique dunes**, which are not at right angles to either summer or winter winds, are formed. Oblique dunes exist only among the Oregon dunes. Starting near the ocean, many of these sand serpents wind gently inland almost 1 mile (1.6 km). Some rise as high as 165 feet (50 m). Each year, they grow longer and bigger.

Why don't other dune systems have oblique dunes? The formation of these long-lived dunes is not completely understood. People who have studied the Oregon dunes know that it takes the particular alternating of summer and winter winds along the Oregon coast to produce this unique dune.

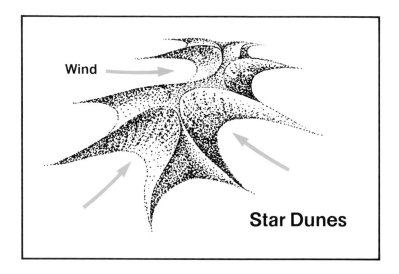

Wind

Star Dunes

Usually, dunes are located in regions where the wind comes from only one direction. The Sahara has northeast trade winds. Southwest winds blow almost constantly in Great Sand Dunes National Monument and in White Sands National Monument. Under such wind conditions, dune formations line up one after another, and they all move in the same direction. When winds blow from many directions, star-shaped dunes are formed. Star-shaped dunes are found in the Gran Desierto and in other regions.

Where sand meets the edge of a forest, as it does in the Oregon dunes some distance from the sea, a **precipitation ridge** is created. When wind carrying sand is deflected upward by the trees, it loses speed and drops its load of sand, creating a ridge.

Another type of formation occurs where the forest edge meets the sand. When the wind blows a hole in the forest vegetation or the vegetation is destroyed by animals, the remaining vegetation acts as an obstacle, blocking the wind from all directions but one. The sand piles up in the open area, forming a curved ridge that is shaped like half of a watermelon. This **parabola dune** is the highest of the Oregon dune formations and is a fairly common formation in other dune areas as well.

24

A precipitation ridge, lined with dead trees, forms where sand and forest meet.

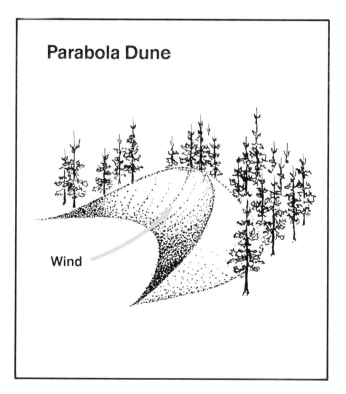

Parabola Dune

Wind

Some dune formations can be heard as well as seen! Dunes may squeak, roar, sing, or boom when disturbed. The sound is determined by the way the sand is disturbed. A passing wind may cause the dunes to hum, buzz, or moan. Digging into a sand dune with a shovel can produce a sound like a short, low note on a cello. Sand dunes may rumble or give off thundering booms when someone walks or drives on their surfaces.

Scientists who have studied the sand grains from "booming" dunes under special microscopes found that the grains must be highly polished, perfectly smooth round balls in order to produce sounds. They must be absolutely dry and are usually especially small grains. Dunes that make noise are usually composed mostly of quartz sand. However, some "booming" dunes in Hawaii are formed from calcite sand.

Dunes that are undisturbed by people display many intriguing textures, tracks, and patterns. Wind is a magnificent sculptor. Wavy patterns are particularly beautiful with sunlight shining on them. The scouring of dune formations by winds during rainstorms gives them a slick appearance. **Cross bedding** occurs where a wind blowing from one direction has formed sand lines that are blown into swirls when the wind changes direction with the season. Sometimes the wind uncovers a rare formation called a **fulgurite**. This is a solid mass created when lightning strikes bare sand, heating and fusing sand particles together.

Does it sound like sand is everywhere? In fact, this Oregon dune area is a wonderful place to study plants. We have seen that vegetation can play a part in the building of some sand formations. Plants play another important part on the Oregon dunes. Some plants are able to take root and prepare the way for future plant growth and perhaps the development of forests.

The growth of **pioneer plants**, or the first plants, changes the soil conditions and other conditions of the plants' immediate environment, which prepares the way for other plants to take over. This continues to happen until a **climax forest** is established. A climax forest is filled with mature trees that are the same species as some of the new seedlings. This growth process from pioneer plants to a climax forest is called **plant succession**.

Plant succession takes place in many different environments. Our discussion of plant succession explains what most often happens in the Oregon dunes and mentions only a few examples of the various plants that are involved in the progression from pioneer plants to climax forest.

The climate on the Oregon coast is mild throughout the year. The mild climate and heavy winter rainfall cause rapid vegetation growth, so a lot happens in a short time, even in one person's lifetime. In this region, we can actually watch plant succession take place.

Rapid plant growth on the Oregon coast makes it possible for us to see the different stages of plant succession.

To anchor them in the sand, beach grasses have deep, spreading roots called rhizomes.

Plant succession in the Oregon dunes can start on bare sand where moisture, sunlight, moderate temperatures, and lack of competition with other plants make it possible for the pioneer plants to grow. These plants, however, must manage to thrive on shifting, blowing sand, must tolerate ocean salt spray and sand burial, and must find nutrients—though they don't need many—necessary for their growth.

Many seedlings sprout in the wet sand, but they don't survive long unless they have good root systems to anchor them. Beach grasses do this by sending **rhizomes**, underground creeping stems, down into the sand. These rhizomes spread out over a large area, anchoring the plants solidly. Even with a lot of tugging, it is hard to pull up beach grasses.

Ocean waves wash ashore organisms, such as seaweed, which decay and are blown inland, providing nutrients for plants.

Some pioneer plants form **hummocks**, clumps of plants that accumulate mounds of sand around them as they catch the blowing grains. Beach grasses, yellow abronia, and silver beach-weed are pioneer plants that form such mounds. However, hummocks are very unstable—they are in a continual state of being built up or eroded away by the wind, and they don't usually start plant succession.

It is not enough for a plant to resist uprooting by the wind and burial by the sand. Plants need nutrients to grow. How do they get these on bare sand? Ocean breezes carry food in the form of tiny organisms and minerals. This food is in the foam of ocean water that you see at the seashore. Also, seaweed and organic litter along the beach decompose and are blown inland to the dunes, providing nutrients for the vegetation.

Pioneer plants, such as beach morning glory, spread creeping stems on the surface of the sand.

Like beach grasses, sea rocket is a pioneer plant that withstands sand burial and salt spray. It spreads quickly over the seaward side of the dunes. Beach pea and beach morning glory, other pioneer plants, spread creeping stems on the surface of the sand. Sea rocket, beach pea, and beach morning glory are only a few of the plants that begin plant succession by **stabilizing** the shifting sands, restricting sand movement. Now, plants that do not tolerate sand burial can grow.

32

Douglas's dune tansy grows in sand that has been enriched by the growth and decay of pioneer plants.

The pioneer plants do more than just stabilize their shifting environment. When they die and decay, the pioneer plants add nutrients to the sand. This sandy soil has a new texture. When you sift it through your fingers, it feels different than pure sand. Besides containing more plant nutrients, this mixture of sand and soil retains water better than pure sand.

Plants that need richer soil thrive on the enriched sand. Yellow-flowered dune tansy and purple-blossomed seashore lupine dot the sandy soil. The pioneer plants give them some protection from the wind and some shading from the sun. The soil continues to improve, and more and more plants spring up. The new environment is unfavorable for the specialized pioneer plants, and they die out as other plants keep growing.

Moss prepares the way for kinnikinnick in one pattern of plant succession.

The chain of growth and replacement continues. In one pattern of succession, moss becomes established and prepares the way for kin kinnick, also called bearberry, to grow up through it. Kinnikir ick is a low, spreading pla t with bright red berries that are foc for some wildlife. The moss dies after the kinnikinnick spreads over it. Eventually, tiny tree seedlings, particularly coast pine, come up through the kinnikinnick. The seedling pines are sheltered from the wind and from sand burial by the earlier plants. By this time, many species have enriched the sand.

Plant succession progresses to a coast pine forest.

Various shrubs now begin to appear. Salal and evergreen huckleberry are common ones, but western rhododendron is the dominant shrub. Douglas fir trees grow among the shrubs. In late spring and early summer, the tall rhododendrons have clusters of large, pink flowers that are beautiful among the green of the Douglas fir and against the gold background of distant sand. This plant succession on the shifting dunes progresses to a coast pine forest and, in time, to a climax forest of hemlock and cedar trees. The climate of the shady, wind-protected forest is much different than that of the open sand.

Monkeyflowers, a type of pioneer plant, grow along the low, wet region of Tenmile Creek.

A different sequence of plant succession takes place in each of the dune environments, from dry, windy beachfronts to moist deflation plains and creek banks. Plant succession in wet areas occurs faster than in dry areas. Numerous pioneer plants grow there because the water so important to their development is available.

Deflation plains have high, dry edges and low spots that are very wet. The areas in between are moist. In dry areas of deflation plains, wild strawberry plants spread out by sending out stems low to the ground. Later, they have white flowers that produce sweet berries. Golden monkeyflowers and twisted orchids are pioneer plants that edge the low, wet regions. Beach grasses and salt rush, which looks somewhat like a grass, begin plant succession in the moist places.

Plant succession in the deflation plains may result in a climax forest of Sitka spruce.

The many pioneer plants of the deflation plains prepare the way for succession to a shrub community—usually coast willow and wax myrtle in the wet places and salal and evergreen huckleberry on the dry edges, but they are often mixed together. The stage is then set for Sitka spruce, a climax forest species of the deflation plains, to grow. Sitka spruce grow well along the coast because they need the salt sprays and mists that float in from the sea. These trees are bent and twisted into strange shapes by the winter winds.

The view from an inland precipitation ridge

The best way to appreciate the Oregon dune landscape is by visiting it. Walking from the seashore to a windy dune top, then to a sheltered valley between sand formations, and finally to the forest edge, lets one feel and see the different plant environments. But explorers need to be observant to avoid getting lost. The sparkle of the ocean or the sound of the surf can be used as a point of reference. In the distance may be a small patch of trees, a forest island that has not yet been buried by the sand.

Dunes all over the world have vegetation that is very specific to the weather and soil conditions of their particular region. The coastal dunes of the eastern United States contain plants and trees that are adapted to the local climate. There, the pattern of plant succession is similar to that of the Oregon dunes but with different vegetation. A beach pea grows there as well as other flowers, such as hardy seaside goldenrod and golden-flowered dusty miller. Poison ivy helps anchor the sand. In the Atlantic coastal dunes, beach plum trees, beech trees, and hickory trees are examples of plants that are a part of coastal succession.

This tall-stemmed yucca plant resists burial in the white gypsum sands of New Mexico.

Would you find the same plants in desert dunes that you would find in coastal dunes? It is not likely. Water is an important factor in plant growth, and deserts get little rain. Because of this lack of moisture, desert plant growth is slow, and there is essentially no plant succession. Like plants on the coast, though, desert plants have to be able to withstand sand burial. One desert plant, the yucca plant, resists burial in white gypsum sands and in other sands by growing a taller and taller stem—up to 40 feet high (12 m).

Plant succession and streams compete with sand movement at Tenmile Creek.

In most dune areas, plant succession competes with sand movement. In the Oregon dunes, sand advances inland 3 to 5 feet (1.0-1.5 m) each year, sometimes more. Sometimes sand will dam the mouth of a stream, turning it into a freshwater lake. Gradually the lake will fill with sand that might, in time, be blown into dunes. Some streams are simply diverted by the advancing sand, taking new paths to the sea. Huge banks of sand edge these waterways.

This dead tree pierces a rippled dune near a precipitation ridge.

When dunes advance on a forest, it is usually a losing battle for the forest as a new precipitation ridge forms farther inland. Skeleton trees tell the story of past burials.

People have tried to alter the path of shifting sands. In the early 1900s, the Oregon dunes were thought troublesome, as they can be when they drift onto roads or bury homes. Early settlers who destroyed the natural dune vegetation that was controlling dune movement were partly to blame for this sand movement.

Beginning in the 1930s, European beach grass, Scotch broom (also from Europe), and coast pine (a native tree) were planted on the Oregon coast to set up a plant succession and stabilize some dune areas. European beach grass grows fast and spreads quickly—especially where the wind is depositing sand along the shoreline. This grass, which grows faster than any of the native plants, has done its job too well. High foredunes, created by European beach grass, threaten to cut off the supply of sand for dune building inland, thus affecting the natural cycle of life in the dune areas. Experts are studying the situation and hope to resolve it. Nature may help to solve the problem, since ferocious winter storms sometimes destroy parts of the foredunes. It is impossible to say how the dunes would look today if people had not tried to change them.

Off-road vehicles erode the dune formations and cause sand to advance faster than is normal.

In recent times, people have urged the protection of some untouched dunes so that they can be enjoyed by all of the people. In 1972, a portion of the Oregon dunes—the Oregon Dunes National Recreation Area—was set aside by the United States Congress for everyone to enjoy. This area includes shifting sands, wildflowers, wildlife, freshwater lakes, creeks, and 42 miles (67 km) of ocean shoreline between the Coos and the Siuslaw rivers.

There are many different ways to enjoy this environment, and people often disagree on how the O.D.N.R.A. should be used. Off-road vehicles—dune buggies, motorcycles, and three-wheelers— are allowed in certain sections. Riding these vehicles is an exciting, though dangerous, way to explore the dunes, but they erode the dune formations and cause the sand to advance even faster than is normal. Sometimes people ride these vehicles into areas where they are not allowed and threaten sensitive plant and animal communities.

Where dunes are produced, wind and sand have combined to make a constantly changing landform. It is important that people enjoy this unique environment in a way that insures its continued development. Left alone to shift according to the patterns of the wind or to stabilize under succeeding vegetation, the dunes are a never-ending resource for study and recreation.